SCIENCE TOOLS

USING MACHINES AND INSTRUMENTS

by Chris Eboch

illustrated by Jon Davis

PICTURE WINDOW BOOKS
Minneapolis, Minnesota

5

0

-5

Thanks to our advisers for their expertise, research, and advice:

Jeffrey R. Pribyl, Ph.D.
Professor of Chemistry and Geology
Minnesota State University, Mankato

Susan Kesselring, M.A., Literacy Educator
Rosemount–Apple Valley–Eagan (Minnesota) School District

Editors: Jacqueline Wolfe and Nick Healy
Designer: Ben White
Page Production: Joseph Anderson
Creative Director: Keith Griffin
Editorial Director: Carol Jones
The illustrations in this book were created digitally.

This book was produced for Picture Window Books by
Bender Richardson White, U.K.

Picture Window Books
5115 Excelsior Boulevard
Suite 232
Minneapolis, MN 55416
877-845-8392
www.picturewindowbooks.com

Printed in the United States of America.

Library of Congress Cataloging-in-Publication Data
Eboch, Chris.
Science tools : using machines and instruments / by Chris Eboch ;
illustrated by Jon Davis.
p. cm. — (Amazing science)
Includes bibliographical references and index.
ISBN-13: 978-1-4048-2199-6 (hardcover)
ISBN-10: 1-4048-2199-6 (hardcover)
1. Scientific apparatus and instruments—Juvenile literature. I. Davis,
Jon, ill. II. Title. III. Series.
Q185.3.E26 2007
502.8—dc22   2006008322

Table of Contents

Your Tools

You can watch a butterfly. You can listen to music. You can smell bread baking. You can feel the sun warming your skin.

You use your senses to explore the world around you. Your eyes, ears, nose, tongue, and skin are your tools.

4

FUN FACT

Close your eyes, and then touch your hair. Your hair moves. You can feel the movement on your scalp. You do not have feeling in your hair. Still, you can feel when something touches you because of your hair.

Tools at Work

Your senses are wonderful tools. However, they are not exact. You can tell it is hot outside, but how hot is it? You can tell the music is loud, but how loud is it?

Scientists can tell us. They make tools that work better than our senses can. We use some of these tools at home. Scientists use other tools for their work.

FUN FACT

Some people cannot use all of their senses. Science may help them. Scientists make tools that help some deaf people to hear and some blind people to see.

Looking Bigger

You can use a magnifying glass or hand lens to study small things. You can see the pattern on a butterfly's wings.

Scientists use microscopes to see tiny things. They can see the patterns in a snowflake. They can even see the germs that make people sick.

FUN FACT

You can get a small microscope to use at home or in school. It can make things appear up to 100 times larger. The best microscopes make things appear 500 million times larger.

Looking Farther

Binoculars help you see things far away. You can watch a bird flying in the distance.

Some people have difficulty seeing far away. Other people cannot focus on close objects. We use a simple tool to fix these problems. We wear eyeglasses.

FUN FACT
A telescope is a tool that helps scientists see far away. They can see stars that are too far away for our eyes alone to see.

Taking Pictures

Machines can record the things we see. You may use a camera to take pictures. Pictures help us remember what we saw.

Infrared cameras take pictures in the dark. They sense heat in objects and produce a picture.

12

FUN FACT

Scientists make tools that take pictures of things we can't even see. At the hospital, a doctor uses an X-ray machine. X-rays make a picture of the inside of the body. The picture shows a person's bones.

Hearing and Sounds

Your ears hear sounds that are quiet or loud. Very loud sounds hurt your ears.

Scientists use sound level meters to measure how loud sounds are. They can measure the loudness of a mouse's squeak, a bell's ring, or an airplane's engine noise.

FUN FACT
You can feel sound. Put your fingers on your throat. Say "hello." You can feel the vibration. All sounds are vibrations.

Sound Recording

You can turn sounds into electrical signals using a microphone. You can turn the electrical signals back into sounds using a loudspeaker. The electrical signals can be used to record and store those sounds.

Scientists have built microphones and loudspeakers into cell phones, computers, music players, and recorders. We use these tools for communication and entertainment.

FUN FACT

Scientists have special microphones that detect sounds our ears cannot hear well. They can be used to record the high squeak of bats screeching. They can be used to record whales singing in the ocean.

In the Air

You can smell food cooking. Smoke detectors also "smell" the air. If they smell smoke, they warn us that there is a fire.

Scientists also use tools to smell the air. They can tell when the air has a lot of pollution. They can warn people to stay inside to avoid air pollution.

FUN FACT

It is hard to taste food if you cannot smell. Have an adult cut a slice of apple and a slice of raw potato. Put on a blindfold and hold your nose. Lick the two foods. They taste the same if you cannot smell them.

19

Hot and Cold

If it feels cold outside, you want to wear a jacket. With a thermometer, you can see how cold it is before you go out. A thermometer measures the air temperature. Scientists have special thermometers for measuring very high temperatures. They can even measure the temperature of lava in a volcano.

We use tools at home. Scientists use tools as well. You have just read about a few of those tools. Can you think of some others?

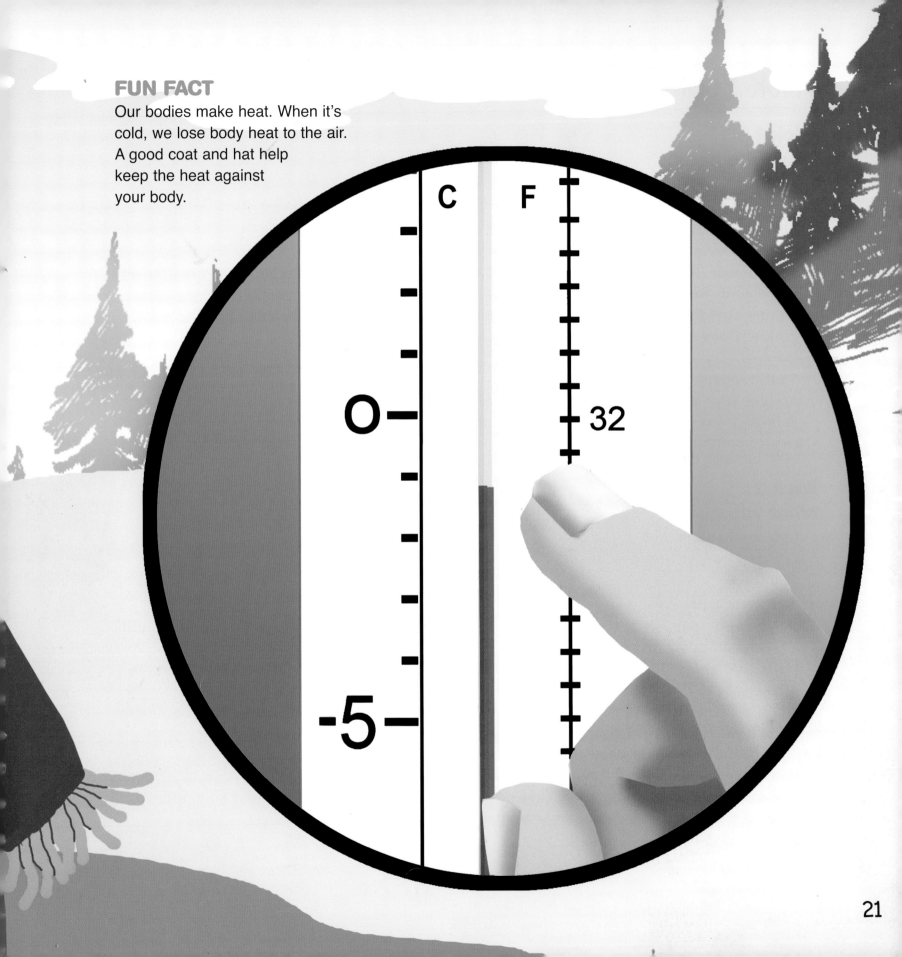

FUN FACT

Our bodies make heat. When it's cold, we lose body heat to the air. A good coat and hat help keep the heat against your body.

C

F

O

-5

32

Trick Your Senses

Trick 1
What you need:

a cardboard tube

What you do:

1. Look through the cardboard tube with your right eye.
2. Hold your left hand in front of your left eye. Hold your hand a few inches away from your eye, with your palm facing you.
3. Look straight ahead with your eyes open. Move your left hand closer to the cardboard tube. Does it look like you have a hole in the side of your hand?

What happened:

Usually, your left and right eyes see almost the same thing. Your brain combines the pictures from your eyes. Here, your left and right eyes see different things. Your brain still tries to combine the pictures. It puts the view through the tube over your hand.

Trick 2
What you need:

a glass of cold water
a glass of water that has been sitting out

What you do:

1. Dip one finger into the cold water. At first it feels cold. Leave it there for a minute, until it doesn't seem so cold.
2. Dip that same finger into the room-temperature water. It feels much warmer than the cold water.
3. Dip a second finger into the room-temperature water at the same time. The first finger feels warm, but the second finger feels cold.

What happened:

Your skin feels changes in heat. Your first finger feels the change between cold and warm. It thinks the warm water is warmer than it really is.

Science Tools Extras

Amazing Skin

You can feel many things with your skin. Touch the things around you. Are they hot or cold? Are they hard or soft? Are they rough or smooth? Push your hands against this page. You can feel pressure. Your skin can even feel pain. Pain warns you to stop what you are doing.

Extraordinary Animal Senses

Many animals have better senses than people do. Dogs can hear sounds that are too high for our ears. A polar bear can smell a seal 12 miles (19 kilometers) away. An eagle can see a rabbit from 1 mile (1.6 km) away. Better senses help these animals survive.

Echoing Bats

Bats have a special sense called echolocation. A bat makes high sounds as it flies. When a sound hits an insect, the sound bounces back, making an echo. The echo bounces back to the bat's ears to help it locate the insect. Even in the dark, the bat can tell where the insect is. Whales and dolphins also use echolocation.

Tasty Senses

When you eat, you use three senses: taste, smell, and touch. Your tongue tastes the food. It tells you if the food is sweet, sour, salty, or bitter. Your nose smells the food. It can smell thousands of different flavors. The skin in your mouth tells you how the food feels. Is it hot or cold? Is it crunchy, squishy, smooth, or slimy?

Glossary

binoculars—a tool used by both eyes at the same time to see distant things

infrared—invisible light that can be seen with a special camera

microphone—a tool that can be used to record sound

microscope—a tool that magnifies small things, making them easier to see

pollution—wastes that are harmful for living things

senses—the abilities that let us experience the world, including sight, hearing, smell, taste, and touch

telescope—a tool that magnifies distant things, such as stars

To Learn More

At the Library

Bullock, Linda. *Looking Through a Microscope.* New York: Children's Press, 2003.

Johnson, Jinny. *Senses.* New York: Kingfisher, 2004.

Richardson, Adele. *Thermometers.* Mankato, Minn.: Capstone Press, 2004.

On the Web

FactHound offers a safe, fun way to find Internet sites related to this book. All of the sites on FactHound have been researched by our staff.

1. Visit *www.facthound.com*
2. Type in this special code for age-appropriate sites: 1404821996
3. Click on the FETCH IT button.

Your trusty FactHound will fetch the best sites for you!

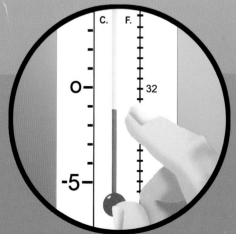

Look for other books in the Amazing Science series:

Composting: Nature's Recyclers
    1-4048-2194-5
Erosion: Changing Earth's Surface
    1-4048-2195-3
Magnification: A Closer Look
    1-4048-2196-1
Science Measurements:
    How Heavy? How Long? How Hot?
    1-4048-2197-X
Science Safety: Being Careful
    1-4048-2198-8